Shoot the Breeze

Shoot th

e Breeze

Sarah Ell

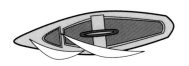

RANDOM HOUSE
NEW ZEALAND

A catalogue record for this book
is available from The National
Library of New Zealand

A RANDOM HOUSE BOOK
published by
Random House New Zealand
18 Poland Road, Glenfield,
Auckland, New Zealand
www.randomhouse.co.nz
First published 2007

ISBN 978 1 86941 908 0

Cover and text design:
Trevor Newman
Printed in China by
Everbest Printing Co Ltd

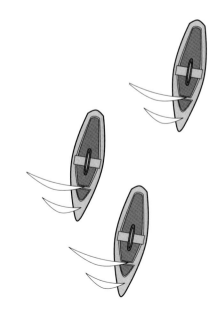

For Rob, who can get away with saying
*Your boat's a pig and you can't park
your grader there*

Introduction

For as long as people have set sail on the seas, there has been nautical language. Even back in the early days of civilisation, when people used rudimentary sailboats for transport and food gathering, there was probably someone yelling *bring that main on!* or *give us a bit of ease, will you!*

With the rise of the military and merchant navy, piracy, sea-borne exploration and long-distance sea voyages, a rich vernacular sprang up which we can identify as being distinctly nautical. It is a uniquely colourful language, evoking the hard but enjoyable life on the ocean wave, from *avast, me hearties* to *three sheets to the wind.*

In more recent times with the rise of recreational sailing, and in particular amateur and professional yacht racing, one branch of salty slang has gained wide currency. Yachtie, a highly specialised, sometimes technical and often somewhat ribald dialect, is spoken worldwide amongst those who sail for fun and competitive satisfaction. It is a complex and diverse tongue, often giving several different names to one manoeuvre or piece of equipment. Largely impenetrable to the uninitiated, Yachtie can appear to be a raft of contradictions, illogical associations, inexplicable connections and sometimes, quite simply, rude jokes. It is a language not easily mastered, and impossible to imitate, but once acquired opens the door to a world of communication hitherto only imagined by the landlubber.

I myself began to learn Yachtie as a teenager, when I discovered I had no idea what my friends who were into sailing were talking about. Perhaps I should have walked away then, but once inducted into this secretive yet fascinating language I became absorbed in its mystery — not to mention deriving hours of pleasure and satisfaction not only from yacht racing, but also endlessly dissecting it in Yachtie afterwards. I was taught Yachtie by native speakers — some, I would claim, of the acknowledged experts in the field, many of whom now compete at an international level as professionals.

As with any living language, Yachtie is a fluid, changing entity, and the best way to keep up with its constant transmogrification is to go sailing, talk sailing, eat and sleep sailing. But for those of you with less time and desire to get wet, those who live or socialise with a Yachtie speaker and wish to understand them better, and those who are merely curious, their interest perhaps piqued by a major event such as the America's Cup, this book is a distilled version: a primer, if you will, in Basic and Advanced Yachtie.

Let's sheet on and hit the line at pace, in clear air . . . *
Sarah Ell

* Bring the sails in and cross the startline with good speed, without another yacht between us and the wind, i.e. the perfect race start.

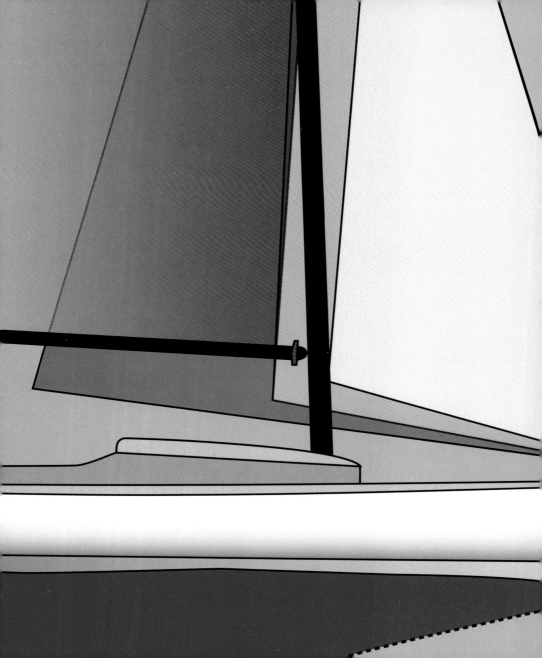

Basic
Yachtie

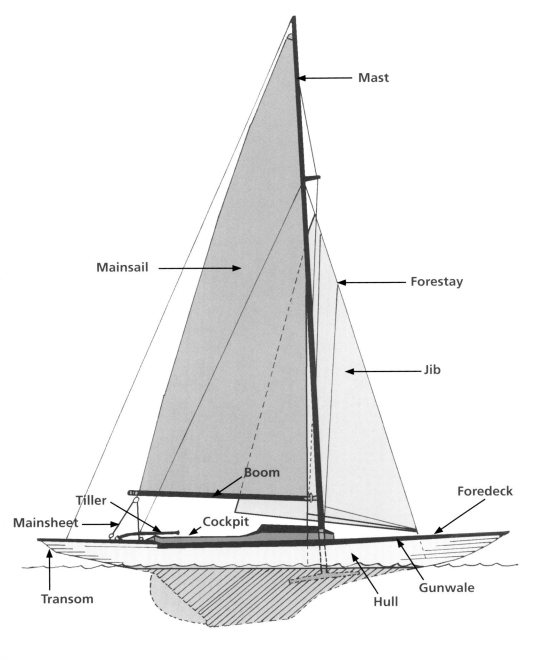

Mast

Mainsail

Forestay

Jib

Boom

Foredeck

Tiller

Mainsheet

Cockpit

Transom

Hull

Gunwale

What goes where?

Parts of the yacht

Yachtie may sometimes seem an illogical language, but by starting with the basics you can build up an understanding of how phrases are put together. For those who are complete novices on the sailing scene, let's start with the very basics.

Bow and stern

The *bow* is the front of the yacht (sometimes called *the pointy end*, but this should only be used by experienced sailors, with irony). The *stern* is the back of the yacht.

Port and starboard

Next, let's clarify the nautical terms for left and right:

port left
starboard right

An easy way to remember this is the phrase 'is there any *port* wine *left?*' Other people remember it by *port* and *left* both being four-letter words. However you choose to remember it, bear in mind that port is the left-hand side of the boat when you are facing the bow. When you are facing the stern, port is on your right.

Simple, eh?

Red and green

So you think you've got that sussed and want to get more technical. The international lights and buoyage system designates port as red and starboard as green, so the *aide-memoire* can be extended to 'is there any *red port* wine *left*?' However, if you need to use a phrase like this to remember the difference between port and starboard, you probably shouldn't be in a position where you are navigating.

Fore and aft

If you are moving towards the bow you are going *forward* (correctly pronounced *for'ard* in a somewhat piratical manner). This concept also appears in words such as *foredeck* (the deck at the front of the yacht), *foresail* (see *jib*, *genoa*, page 27), and *forward hand* (another name for *bowman*).

You'd think, therefore, that if you were moving toward the stern that you would be going backward? Of course not, that would be too logical. If you are moving towards the stern, you are going *aft*. Again, aft crops up in expressions such as *afterguard* (the 'brains trust' at the back of a racing boat) and *aft double grunter* (the double *berth* under the *cockpit*).

Beam

The widest part of the boat, usually in the middle. Used as a point of reference, as in *We were abeam of the other yacht* or *The wind was forward of the beam*.

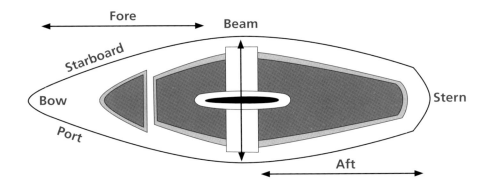

Parts of the yacht

Bailer Container used to bail water out of the *cockpit* or, in the worst case scenario, the *cabin*. Something you hopefully won't have to use, but Team New Zealand thought that in 2005 and look where it got them.

Berth A bed, of sorts. Unless you're in superyacht territory, these are likely to be too narrow, somewhat salty and permanently damp.

Bilge Where the bottom of the boat meets the *topsides*. The *bilges* are the lowest internal part of the hull, hence the expressions *bilge water, bilge rat* and *pump the bilge,* which can also be a euphemism for urination.

Block A pulley or pulleys enclosed in a casing, through which *sheets*, *halyards* and other control lines are run. A *snatch block* sounds nasty but is just one that can be opened up and clipped onto a line, rather than the line being threaded through it. Some blocks contain ratchets, angled teeth on the pulley that make the line easy to pull in but hard to ease out; these are called *ratchet blocks* (not be confused with *ratshit blocks*, i.e. ones that are no good and need to be replaced).

Cabin The interior of the yacht. Depending on

the size of the yacht and its purpose — i.e. racing or cruising — it can vary from black and completely empty (like on an America's Cup boat) to plush and extremely comfortable. Entering the cabin is referred to as *going (down) below*. Fluent Yachtie speakers never say *going downstairs*.

Cabintop The bit in the middle of the yacht that sticks up so you can stand up in the *cabin*. The *keyboards* are usually positioned here.

Cleat A fitting which holds a *sheet* or line in position. Different types include *clam cleats*, which have sprung jaws to hold the line, and the *bum cleat*, which is when someone is sitting on the line.

Clutch See *jammer*

Coaming The vertical side of the *cabin* between the *cabintop* and the *side decks*.

Cockpit The open area at the back of the yacht, from which it is steered.

Companionway The opening that leads from the *cockpit* to the *cabin*. While it might seem like a convenient and comfortable place to position yourself, out of harm's way, remember the nautical expression *Only admirals and arseholes stand in companionways*.

Donk The engine. Possibly short for donkey, because it does all the work. The engine can also be called the *iron mainsail*.

There's no wind, we may as well use the iron mainsail.
Galley The kitchen.
Gunwale Where the *deck* meets the *topsides*. See *gunwale bum*.

Gunwale bum

This is the name given to the excruciating itching of the buttocks and upper thighs caused by salt or sweat drying on the skin (usually beneath wet weather gear). Absolutely unable to be assuaged by actual scratching, the only cure appears to be sitting completely still until the itching subsides, or getting your bum wet again. Also called *yachtie bottie* or *IBS* (Itchy Bottom Syndrome).

Head The toilet. So named because in the early days of sailing ships, the 'seats of ease' — basically just holes in the ship's side railing — were positioned up the front of the ship (at its head). As these ships could only sail downwind, any unsavoury aromas would be blown away from the rest of the crew. Nowadays the head is usually still placed in the forward part of the boat, and unsavoury aromas created there are even less tolerated.

Jammer (US *rope clutch*) A device for securing *halyards* or control lines whereby the rope in question runs through a tube and a handle is lowered to lock it off. Usually positioned in banks on the *keyboards*, where the crew can clip their knees on them when moving about the *cabintop*.

Keel Appendage attached to the hull below the water which gives the yacht stability; in very basic terms, it stops the boat being blown over when its sails fill with wind. Comprised of a vertical *fin* with a lead *bulb* on the bottom. There is also a current fashion for racing yacht keels to be *canting*, which means they can be angled from side to side to increase stability.

Keyboards (US *pit*) A bank of *cleats* or *jammers* on the *cabintop*, from which the various *halyards* and control lines (e.g. the *cunningham*) are controlled. Also a crew position (see page 41).

Lifelines A cheerful name for the wires which enclose the deck and keep the crew from falling overboard to their deaths. Some racing yachts, including America's Cup yachts, don't have lifelines, leaving their crews to take their chances. They also serve to cut you in half when sitting on the side of the boat during a race, as they are never at a comfortable height or tension.

Painter A rope attached to the bow of a boat, used to tie it to a wharf or to another boat, in the case of the *tender*.

Pick The anchor.

Go forward and pull up the pick.

Pit See *keyboards*

Primaries See *winches*

Pulpit Not the area from which the skipper preaches to the crew. The metal railing which encloses the deck at the *bow*. In one of the more logical extensions of Yachtie, the corresponding railing at the back of the yacht is called the *pushpit*. Clever, eh?

Pushpit See *pulpit*

Rail See *toerail*

Rope clutch See *jammer*

Rubber ducky See *tender*

23

Rudder Appendage below the water controlled by the *tiller* or *wheel*, which steers the yacht. Some racing yachts have a second rudder forward of the *keel*, ostensibly to improve control, which is called a *canard*. This is also the French word for duck. Go figure.

Side decks The decks running down the sides of the yacht on either side of the *cabintop*.

Stanchions Upright metal posts through which the *lifelines* are run.

Tender A dinghy or small boat belonging to a yacht, used for going ashore or to other boats for parties. The large inflatables used by America's Cup teams as support boats can also be called tenders, and sometimes *rubber duckies*.

Tiller The horizontal bar attached to the *rudder* with which the boat is steered. Also called *the stick* (and thus the helmsman can be nicknamed *the dick on the stick*). May have a tiller *extension* fitted to it to enable the helmsman to steer from the side of the *cockpit*. See also *wheel*

Toerail A raised lip or metal rail around the edge of the boat at the *gunwale*. Notoriously uncomfortable to sit on during long races. Leads to the expressions *sitting on the rail* and *rail weight* (see page 43).

Topsides The upper part of a boat's hull, from the

What do you call the knob on the end of the tiller that steers the yacht?
The helmsman.

waterline up to the deck. The underneath part is just called the bottom, not the bottomsides, however.

Transom The flat surface at the *stern* of the yacht. Sometimes also used to refer unflatteringly to a person's backside.

She's got a bit of a wide transom.

Tumblehome 1. Something you're liable to do after a few too many rums at the yacht club. 2. A yacht-design term describing the curve of a yacht's hull. Hull shape can also be described in terms of *sheer*, *flare* and *flam* (only by the very experienced).

Wheel Larger yachts are steered with a wheel or pair of wheels, kind of like a bus. See *tiller*

Winches Used to supply the resistance and power to pull on *sheets* and control lines. The pair of larger winches on each side of the cockpit can also be called *primaries*. Winches can be *two-speed* (meaning they operate in a different gear depending on which way you wind them) or *self-tailing*, where the sheet is held in place in a groove at the top of the winch when grinding.

Winch handle Removable handle that clips into the top of a winch when grinding is required. Can also be used to take the caps off beer bottles.

Is it a boat or a yacht?

The two terms are somewhat interchangeable. Yachtie speakers tend to refer to yachts as boats, as in *Meet you down at the boat* or *We didn't see the other boat until we just about hit it.* Americans tend to call small yachts *sailboats*. *Yacht* is also used as a verb, as in *We're just going out for a yacht.* There are also different types of yachts. Small sailing boats that can be put on a trailer are called *dinghies*. Larger boats with weighted centreboards that can be raised and lowered for transporting are called *trailer sailers* or, if they're more performance-oriented, *sportsboats*. Boats with fixed lead keels are called *keelboats*, and yachts with more than one hull (*catamarans and trimarans*) are called, naturally, *multihulls*.

Sails and rigging fundamentals

The *mast*, *boom* and other items fixed in position are known as the *standing rigging*. The fact that it is called *standing* implies that it is best kept upright, which sadly some sailors seem to forget.

Sheets, *halyards*, sail-control lines and other adjustable bits of string are known as *running rigging.* That's why they get sworn at when they don't run freely.

Boom The horizontal pole attached at right angles to the mast, to which the *foot* of the *mainsail* is attached. The old Yachtie joke is that it is called the boom because of the noise it makes when it hits you in the head. If this were true, it would be more likely to be called the *sickening crack.*

Halyard Rope attached to the top corner of a sail to hoist it up the *mast*. Known by the names of the sails e.g. *main halyard*, *gennaker halyard*. Nautically pronounced *hal*-yid.

Jib The smaller, triangular sail flown in front of the mast and used largely for sailing upwind. Also called the *headsail*, *foresail* or *genoa*, although strictly speaking, a jib is a foresail which is set in front of the mast only, while the *luff* of a genoa overlaps the mainsail, in which case it can

Parts of the sail

The three corners of a sail are named the *head* (at the top), *tack* (the forward lower corner) and *clew* (the aft lower corner). *Spinnakers* have a head and two clews (because they have a sheet attached to both lower corners). The three edges of a sail also have names: the *leech* is the leading edge (attached to the forestay or the mast), the *luff* is the free-flying aft edge, and the *foot* runs along the bottom. The unpleasant-sounding *roach* is the area of the sail outside a diagonal line from the end of the *boom* to the top of the *mast.*
They've got a real roachy main.

Let's go fly a kite

Hoisted sails, like flags, are referred to as being flown. *We decided to fly the gennaker.* Hoisting the spinnaker is known as *flying the kite.* The sails being flown by a yacht can also collectively be known as *rag. We had a fair bit of rag up.*

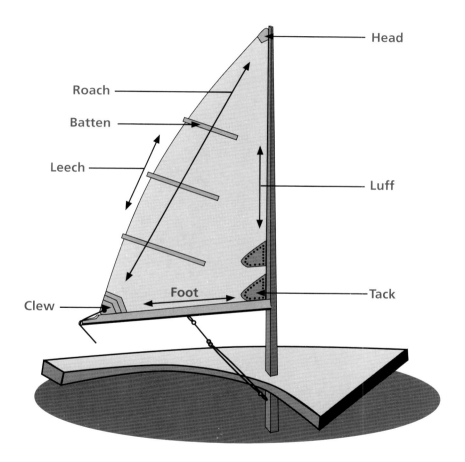

What goes where?

Head

Roach

Batten

Leech

Luff

Clew

Foot

Tack

be known as an *overlapper*. Its shape is controlled by the *jib sheets* or *genoa sheets*. A racing yacht's headsails are often known by number, i.e. *number one*, *number two* etc, with the number one the largest sail. See also *code zero*, *jibtop*

Mainsail The main sail of the boat (I can't put it any more simply than that!). The position of the mainsail is controlled by the *mainsheet*, and its shape fine-tuned by the *vang*, *cunningham* and *outhaul*.

Mast The metal or composite pole in the middle of the yacht that holds the sails up. Sometimes called the *stick* or just the *rig*. The unlikely event of it breaking is known as *dismasting*, or by the gentle-sounding euphemism *dropping the rig*.

They were doing OK until they dropped the rig.

Sheets There are no 'ropes' on a yacht. Ropes that are used to control the sails are called sheets e.g. *mainsheet*, *genoa sheet*, *spinnaker sheet*. To gain the appearance of a fluent Yachtie speaker, learn to refer to the sheets by their correct names (i.e. by the sail they control), rather than 'that blue rope' or 'the pink and white bit of string by your foot', unless you are dealing with someone less experienced than yourself and yelling 'grab that sheet' will have them looking around for the laundry basket. Note: *sheet* is also a verb, meaning to bring in or 'sheet on' a sail.

Spinnaker A large, lightweight sail flown in front of the mast, used for sailing downwind. Sometimes called by the inexperienced the *coloured sail*. Also called the *kite*, *chute* or *bag*, or referred to by the weight of sailcloth it is made out of e.g. *half-ounce, three-quarter*. Spinnakers may be *masthead*, where the *halyard* runs to the top of the mast, or *fractional,* where it comes out part-way up the mast. See also *gennaker*

Other bits and pieces

Asymmetric See *gennaker*

Bag See *spinnaker*

Barberhaulers See *tweakers*

Battens Thin, flexible lengths of timber, fibreglass or other composites inserted into pockets in the *mainsail* and sometimes the *genoa*, to encourage optimum sail shape. Inserted and removed with the aid of a *batten poker*.

Brace When the *spinnaker* is hoisted, one of the two ropes attached to it is used to adjust its shape (the *spinnaker sheet*), and the other runs through the outside end of the *spinnaker pole* and is used to move it fore and aft. This is called the *brace*, or *guy*. When the yacht changes direction downwind, the spinnaker pole is swapped to the other side, the sheet becomes the brace, and the brace becomes the sheet. Simple, eh? Some yachts are set up with two ropes clipped to each *clew* of the spinnaker, so there is a sheet and a brace on both sides. In this instance, the rope on the sheet side that is not being used is called the *lazy brace* or *lazy guy*, and the rope on the brace side that is not in use is called the *lazy sheet.*

Chute See *spinnaker*

Code Zero This very James Bond-sounding type of headsail initially came to prominence in the round-the-world race, where they were used for *tight reaching* (see page 66). These huge sails can sometimes be bigger than the *mainsail*, and are a cross between a very large *jib* and a *gennaker*.

Cunningham Control line attached to the *tack* of the *mainsail*, used to adjust the shape of the sail by pulling down the *leech*. Also called, by some smartarses, the *smart pig* (work it out).

Downhaul Control line attached to the underside of the *spinnaker pole,* used in conjunction with the *spinnaker topping lift* to adjust the height of the pole, and stop it from *skying* (see *vang*). Also inexplicably called the *downf*cker*.

Foresail See *jib*

Fractional See *spinnaker*

Gennaker An asymmetric *spinnaker*, flown with its *tack* fixed to a *prod* and both *sheets* attached to the single *clew*. Used for *reaching* downwind, rather than *running* (see Points of sail, page 64).

Genoa See *jib*

Gooseneck The fitting attaching the *boom* to the *mast*.

Guy See *brace*

Half-ounce See *spinnaker*

Headsail See *jib*

Iron mainsail See *donk* (page 21)

Jibtop A very large *headsail* which is sheeted outside the yacht's sidestays, so is useful for *tight reaching* (see Points of sail, page 64). Also sometimes called a *reacher*.

Jockey pole See *whisker pole*

Kicker See *vang*

Kicking strap See *vang*

Kite See *spinnaker*

Lazy guy The crewmember who does the least work. See also *brace*

Lazy sheet What Australians call the crewmember who does the least work. See also *brace*

Mail topper See *topping lift*

Mainsheet Sheet used to trim the *mainsail.*

Masthead See *spinnaker*

Number one See *jib*

Outhaul Control line attached to the *clew* of the *mainsail,* used to adjust the shape of the sail by pulling along the *foot.*

Overlapper See *jib*

Pole See *spinnaker pole*

Pole topper See *topping lift*

Prod See *spinnaker pole*

Reacher See *jibtop*

Rig See *mast*

Spinnaker pole Also known as the *spinnaker boom.* A portable tube, one end of which attaches to the mast and the other supports one of the corners of the *spinnaker* when sailing downwind. Boats which use an asymmetrical spinnaker or *gennaker* may instead have a fixed or retractable *prod.* This is worth knowing to avoid misunderstanding and possible embarrassment when someone asks you to *get the pole up* or *get the prod out*

34

(see also *Did they say that out loud?*, page 124).

Spinnaker topping lift See *topping lift*

Stick See *mast*

Storm trysail A very very small *jib.*

Tackline Control line used to pull the *tack* of the *gennaker* out to the end of the *prod*, when hoisting. Contrary to what you might expect, when someone calls *tack!* during the gennaker hoist, this does not mean the boat is about to change direction, it means *pull on the tackline.*

Telltales Small pieces of wool or thread or strips of fabric attached to the sails to indicate their shape relative to the wind. The telltales will fly smoothly and horizontally on both sides of the sail when the wind flow across it is optimal. Also called *woollies.*

Three-quarter See *spinnaker*

Topper See *topping lift*

Topping lift Also called *topper.* Most larger yachts have two toppers: the *main topping lift*, a line which runs from the top of the *mast* to the end of the *boom*, and is used to stop the boom falling into the *cockpit* when the *mainsail* is not hoisted, and the *spinnaker topping lift*, or *pole topper*, which is used in conjunction with the *downhaul* to adjust the height of the *spinnaker pole.*

Trapeze In order to balance their large sail areas, some dinghies and sportsboats have *trapeze lines* running from the mast. The crew wear special harnesses that hook onto clips on these lines, and they push themselves out to a standing position on the *gunwale*, supported by the trapeze. This gets their weight further over the side of the boat and stops the boat tipping over — usually! Also called *wires*, so the act of sailing this way is called *wiring* or *trapezing*.

Traveller Pulley system running across the boat's *cockpit*, used to adjust the sheeting position of the *mainsheet*.

Trysail A very small *jib*. See *storm trysail*.

Tweakers Small blocks through which the spinnaker sheet and brace are run. Also called *barberhaulers*

Vang Control line attached to the underside of the *boom*, used to adjust the shape of the mainsail. Stops the end of the boom from *skying* (lifting up) when going downwind. Also called the *kicking strap* or *kicker*.

Whisker pole A smaller pole used to hold the *spinnaker brace* off the *lifelines* when *tight reaching*. Also called the *jockey pole*.

Wires See *trapeze*

Woollies See *telltales*

Stay!

The pieces of metal rod and wire which hold the mast in place are collectively called *stays*, perhaps because they make the mast *stay* upright. There are lots of different types of stay; here are a few terms you may encounter: *forestay*, *backstay*, *running backstays* (also called *runners* or *running backs*), *topmast backstay*, *sidestays*, *shrouds*, *lowers*, *Ds*, *diagonals*, *Vs*, *jumpers*, *babystays*, *checkstays*.

Spreaders Horizontal bars jutting out from the mast through which the stays run. These help to stabilise the rigging.

Hounds Where the stays attach to the mast.

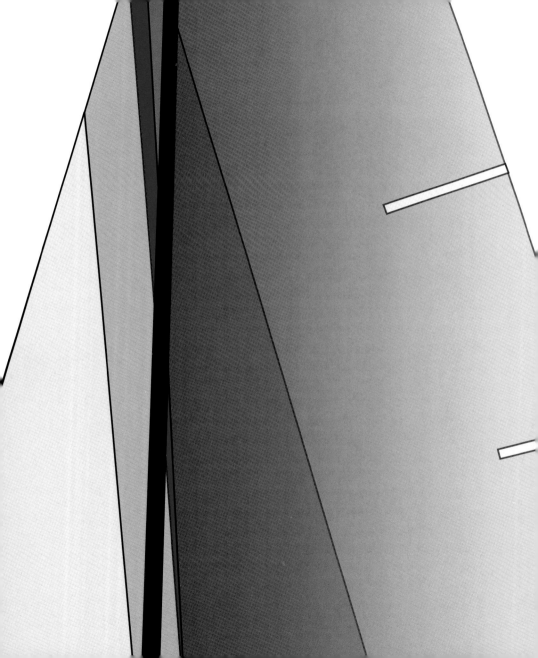

Who does what?

Crew positions and roles

Especially when racing, a yacht is most easily sailed by experienced crewmembers in certain positions, carrying out specific tasks. On an average-sized keelboat there are six key positions, although on smaller boats or when sailing short-handed (with fewer crew than normal), several of these positions can be combined. On larger boats, as in the America's Cup, the main positions can be broken up into sub-positions, and given fancy names.

40

Sexist language

Ladies, a word about sexism. While things have come a long way since 'ladies racing' meant a woman was allowed to helm the boat unless it was starting, finishing, tacking, gybing or going around a mark (and female sailors couldn't be members of many yacht clubs), some apparently sexist terminology still lingers on in Yachtie. Positions on the boat are usually suffixed with the term '-man' (e.g. helmsman, bowman). In some situations the suffix '-chick' may be substituted (e.g. bowchick), but it's OK to put your foot down over the use of 'bitch' (unless you're using it yourself, talking to one of your male crewmembers).

Crew positions

Bowman The bowman (also known as the *forward hand* or *foredeck crew*), looks after goings-on at the front of the boat. These brave and hardy souls deal with the forward sails (*genoa*, *spinnaker* etc), including the deployment of the *spinnaker pole*. The bowman also calls time and distance before the start of a race, signalling to those at the back of the boat how far it is to the startline.

It takes a special kind of person to do the bow, and once your crewmembers have discovered that you know what you're doing, you'll be lucky if they ever let you come back to the cockpit.

As a result of a slight us-and-them mentality, those working up in *Frontierland* may form a community of interest called the *bowmen's union* or *forward-of-the-mast club*.

Mastman A bit of a grunt job, involving pulling up the *halyards* on the mast to hoist sails. The mastman also backs up the bowman during spinnaker-pole manoeuvres.

Keyboards A position the Americans call *pit*. This person deals with the bank of *halyards* and control lines on the cabintop, pulling them on and easing them off as required. So called perhaps because the crewmember in question can end up 'playing' them frantically as they pull on the *topping lift*, ease out the *downhaul*, tail the *spinnaker halyard*, blow the *genoa halyard* and ease some *vang*, *cunningham* and *outhaul*, all within seconds of rounding the *top mark*.

Trimmer The shape or trim of the forward sails is adjusted by one or more trimmers. If there are plenty of crew, different sailors may trim the *genoa* upwind and the *spinnaker* or *gennaker* downwind, but it is often the same person.

Tailer The trimmer is often assisted by a *tailer*, who pulls the sheet in initially and keeps weight on it while the trimmer operates the winch to finish winding it in. Sometimes a pair of crew will alternate trimming and tailing duties, especially if the yacht is engaged in a tiring *tacking duel* (see page 103).

On larger keelboats such as those used in the America's Cup, the physical side of trimming is done by *grinders*, pairs of gorillas — oh, sorry: large, fit sailors — who use upright winches or *coffee grinders* to bring the sails in.

Mainsheet trimmer Trims the *mainsheet* (see, you're getting the hang of this now!). The mainsheet, controlling the *mainsail*, provides much of the 'power' to the yacht, so this is a critical position.

Helmsman The person steering the boat. Sometimes known as *the dick on the stick* if the yacht has a *tiller*, or *the bus driver*, if it's got a *wheel*. The action of steering the boat is sometimes called *steering,* as you might expect, but more correctly *helming.* The person helming is not necessarily called the *skipper*; that expression denotes the person with overall responsibility for the yacht.

Some America's Cup teams will employ a *starting helmsman,* usually someone highly experienced in the hand-to-hand battle that is *match racing* (see page 97). Often the closest part of an America's Cup match will occur in the *pre-start,* and once the starting helmsman has manoeuvred the yacht into the best possible position at the start gun, they hand over to another helmsman who might be better at steering the boat in a straight line.

Rail weight Another very important, some would say vital, job. This role forms most people's introduction to keelboat sailing. Believe it or not, it is important to the performance of most boats to have people sitting on the rail, swapping sides when the boat tacks or gybes.

Should you find yourself in this role, as well as making a contribution to boatspeed, you are in an excellent position to observe native Yachtie speakers first hand and gain exposure to the lingo.

Floater A person not assigned to a particular job, but who helps out where required.

43

The afterguard

In racing situations, and on larger boats such as America's Cup class yachts, there may be additional crewmembers in the cockpit making decisions about where the yacht should sail (*calling tactics*). There may be one or more *tacticians*, including the *heads-up tactician*, who is looking at competing yachts and what is going on elsewhere on the race course. There may also be a *navigator*, whose job it is to crunch performance numbers and pick the best course. This brains trust, gathered comfortably in the cockpit, is known as the *afterguard*.

If you are lucky enough to score yourself a cushy position back here, don't waste your time being paranoid that those know-it-alls up the pointy end are critiquing your every move. Just accept it: they are. What they won't be doing is planning a mutiny, however: they know you could never do their job so they're quite happy to stay where they are and talk about how they'd do yours. It is also worth remembering the Yachtie saying *Boatspeed makes great tacticans of us all*, i.e. if the boat is going fast, all your tactical calls look good.

America's Cup positions

America's Cup yachts are sailed by 17 highly specialised crew. Additional positions you may hear mentioned are:

Midbowman Assists the bowman and mastman on deck during sail changes. May also run the *sewer.*

Sewer An appropriately named job. Involves being largely below decks, packing and stowing sails, preparing them for hoisting and dropping. The inside of a carbon-fibre racing boat is a) black and b) wet and possibly c) stinky, hence the name. A strong stomach is needed for this position.

Runners Some larger racing yachts have a complicated rigging system involving *running backstays*, wires on adjustable pulleys which basically pull the mast backwards and stop it from falling over the front on the boat. In the America's Cup one member of the afterguard will be responsible for letting one runner off and bringing the other side on every time the yacht tacks or gybes. They also help with tactics.

Traveller Adjusts the mainsheet *traveller* and contributes to the 'brains trust' of the afterguard.

17th man A special position invented for the rich owners of America's Cup syndicates. The 17th man on an America's Cup crew is just along for the ride: they get to stand down the back, but are not allowed to touch anything or say anything. They are, however, allowed to write big cheques.

The Crew

1. Bowman
2. Midbowman
3. Sewer
4. Mastman
5. Keyboards/pitman

6/7. Grinders
8/9. Trimmers
10. Mainsail grinder
11. Navigator
12. Mainsail trimmer

13. Helmsman
14. Traveller
15. Tactician
16. Runners
17. 17th man

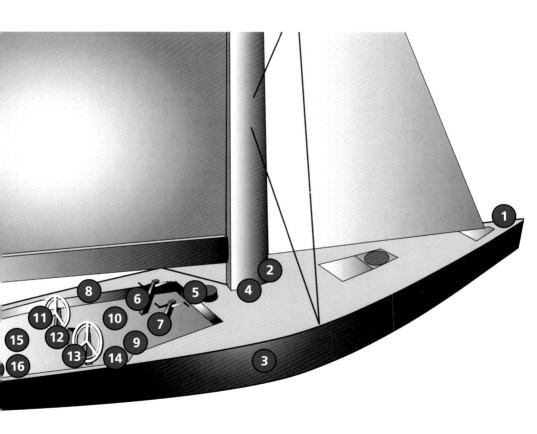

What's in a name?

With the Yachtie's love of alternative names and slang, it stands to reason that no fluent speaker of Yachtie is ever known by their real name. Sailors who meet outside the yacht club are often astounded to discover that the person they know only as *Podgy* or *Blue* is actually called Richard or Ian.

Nicknames are seldom kind or flattering. No one is ever nicknamed *Sexy* or *Clever* (except with irony). They usually end with a vowel and in their simplest form they involve shortening or adding a letter or two to the person's original name e.g. Davo, Mikey, Bazza. In their more complex forms they may refer to a physical or personality trait, or something stupid the person once did. I have sailed with people known as Gimpy, Scuba, Jabber, Ryno, Sherman, Gappy, Nana, Virgil, Ob and Crusty. Don't ask why.

You may also hear Yachties call people the following:

Barry Derogatory term for someone who can't sail (sometimes used in the phrase *Barry goes boating*).

Lemon See *Barry*

Racer chaser Derogatory term for women who hang around the yacht club trying to pick up *rock stars*. For some reason there isn't a matching term for men who hang around at women's regattas — oh yes, it's because there aren't any.

Rock star A pro yachtie, or someone who acts like one.

Show pony A *rock star* who seems more interested in looking good than doing much work on board.

Trolley dolly Derogatory term for a girlfriend or wife of a dinghy sailor, whose role in life seems to be waiting around at the yacht club and bringing her partner's yacht trailer to the water's edge when he comes in from a race. Again, no male equivalent. Hmm.

Yachts are also susceptible to being nicknamed. As it is bad luck to change the name of a boat (see *Superstitions* on page 79–81), owners need to be very careful what they call their yacht and think thoroughly through what *other* people might refer to it as. Yachtie speakers also use the following terms:

Dog A slow yacht.

Grader A slow and heavy keelboat that displaces a lot of water.

Lead mines What multihull sailors call keelboats.

Pig A slow or ugly yacht.

Pup A smaller *dog*.

Rafts What keelboat sailors call multihulls.

Your boat's a pig and you can't park your grader there.

What's it like?

Weather and sea conditions

There can be no sailing without two things: wind and water (unless you're on an ice yacht, but even that involves water of a kind). Consequently there are many Yachtie terms relating to the weather and sea conditions.

Wind

Apparent wind The direction and strength of the wind as it appears while the yacht is in motion. For example, if the yacht is sailing downwind in 10 knots of wind, at a speed of 5 knots, the wind speed on board will feel like only 5 knots. Conversely, if the same boat was sailing upwind, it would feel like there was more than 10 knots of breeze because the forward motion of the yacht is also generating its own breeze. Also referred to as breeze *over the deck*. See also *true wind*

> *We've got 10 knots true and 15 knots over the deck now we're on the wind.*

Blow A term for the wind — but one to use carefully around significant others and non-sailors. Coming home red-faced and glowing, announcing that you 'got a good blow' at sailing is likely to result in you receiving another good blow — around the head. However, there can be no sailing without wind, and a good blow is what all yachties want.

Breeze Even if it's blowing a gale, the hardened yachtie refers to the wind as *breeze*. While your average landlubber thinks of breeze as a gentle zephyr on a summer's day, with typical understatement the yachtie will comment dryly *Bit* *of breeze today* when conditions are approaching Cyclone Bola proportions. The helmsman and trimmers will often ask the crew to either *spot the breeze* (look for where the wind is blowing the strongest), which can be quite confusing for the novice who a) knows the wind is invisible and b) assumes it is all around them. Giving the *afterguard* information on wind strength is called *calling the breeze*, which is not the same as *shooting the breeze*, although on particularly fickle or *puffy* days you might feel like it. Yachties call *puff on* or *pressure on* when a gust of wind is about to reach the yacht.

Bullet A short, sharp *puff*.

Clear air The opposite of *dirty air.*

Crapping out The wind dying (as in *the breeze is crapping out*). For some mysterious reason, the wind never craps back in.

Dirty air Disturbed airflow over the sails of a yacht, caused by another yacht sailing between it and the breeze. Also known, less poetically, as *shit* or *gas.* The opposite, and the ideal, is *clear* (not clean) *air.*

We can't go on sailing in their shit.

We are getting gassed here — let's tack.

Flat spot See *hole*

Fluctuating breeze Wind varying in strength.
See *shifting breeze*

Gas See *dirty air*

Gust See *puff*

Header See *shift*

Hole An area of no breeze. The idea is to keep away from these. Also called a *flat spot.*

We fell into a hole.

We sailed into an area where there was little or no breeze.

We parked it in a hole.

We came to a halt in an area where there was little or no breeze.

We stuck it in a hole.

We sailed purposefully into an area where there was little or no breeze.

Huey Huey is the name given to the mythical god of wind and water conditions, who is alternately invoked (*Let's hope Huey gives us a decent breeze*) and damned (*Bloody Huey*).

Knock See *shift*

Knots Nautical measurement of wind strength (and boat speed). One knot equals one nautical mile per hour

(1.852 kilometres per hour). For a rough conversion, double a measurement in knots to get a speed in kph (see *Beaufort Scale* pages 58–59).

Lift See *shift*

Light Officially, according to the *Beaufort scale* (see pages 58–59), light winds are between 4 and 6 knots. However, *light* is more loosely used to mean a general lack of any decent breeze. In one of the more logical connections of Yachtie, the opposite of light isn't dark, but it is heavy, as in *We're in for some heavy weather.*

Lull An area of less wind. The opposite of a *puff* or *gust.* See also *hole.*

Pressure Something you feel under when you first start sailing and everyone seems to be yelling at once. Also, pressure is another name for the wind, so called because of the force it exerts in the sails. Pressure can be a good thing, and lack of pressure is a bad thing, not just because a little stress is good for us. *No pressure* means no wind, and no wind means no sailing.

Good pressure in the kite.

There is plenty of wind filling the spinnaker.

Puff A gust of wind of varying strength and duration e.g. a small puff, a big puff, a sharp puff. Also a verb, e.g. *It was puffing up to 15 knots.* Conditions can be described as *puffy* if the breeze is fluctuating in strength. Note: Try to avoid saying, *It was a bit puffy last night* in front of a) your doctor and b) your non-sailing partner.

Shift A change in wind direction. If it changes in direction so that a yacht is sailing more directly towards the mark (a good thing), it is called a *lift* and the boat is said to be *lifted.* If the change means the yacht has to sail further away from the mark (a bad thing), this is a *knock* and the boat has been *knocked.* Also known as a *header* (being *headed*). The good news about knocks is, if you *tack* on them they become *lifts.*

I think we should stay on this tack, we're being lifted.

Shifting breeze Wind varying in direction. If it is moving back and forth it is said to be *oscillating.* If it is moving in one direction only it is said to be *tracking.*

That breeze has been tracking right all day.

Shifty The similarity between this word and *shitty* is more than coincidental. It means a breeze which is frequently changing direction, conditions which some sailors find challenging and exhilarating but most find to be just a pain in the arse. Particularly frustrating when paired with *light.*

Sucking the kumara In general, not doing very well.
With regard to the wind, being in an area of no or
unfavourable wind.

We're totally sucking the kumara here.
We've sailed right into a kumara patch.

Tracking See *shifting breeze*

True wind The actual wind speed and direction. See
apparent wind

Wind shadow An area of *light* or no wind immediately
downwind of a large object such as a headland, container
ship or a competing yacht.

How many ways can you say windy?

Blowy	*Fresh*
Breezy	*Heavy*
Blowing a gale	*Honking*
Blowing dogs off chains	*Howling*
Blowing a bastard	*Puffy*
Blowing forty bastards	*Pumping*
Blowing its tits off	*Stiff*
Cranking	*Brisk*

The Beaufort scale

The Beaufort scale is a system of classifying wind strength.
Yachties tend to use a broader, less scientific system, but
here is the conversion from knots, to metrics, to Beaufort
— to Yachtie.

Wind speed (knots)	Wind speed (kph)
0	0
1–3	1.8–5.6
4–6	7.2–10.8
7–10	12.6–18
11–16	19.8–28.8
17–21	30.6–37.8
22–27	39.6–48.6
28–33	50.4–59.4
34–40	61.2–72
41–47	73.8–84.6
48–55	86.4–99

Beaufort force	Yachtie
0	*Useless*
1	*Not worth going out*
2	*You can't start a race in this*
3	*OK breeze*
4	*Decent breeze*
5	*Good breeze*
6	*Fresh*
7	*Getting up there*
8	*Pretty bloody windy*
9	*Blowing 40 bastards*
10	*Blowing dogs off chains*

59

Water

Chop Short, sharp waves.

Green ones Waves. See *white caps*
We were taking a few green ones over the bow.

Green room The sea. Originally a surfing term, but may be used by excitable commentators.
It's a beautiful day out here in the green room.

Hosing Refers to the tide running strongly. Also *pouring* or *pissing*.
The tide's pissing in.

Liquid Himalayas Coined by yachting commentator *par excellence* Pete Montgomery to describe conditions experienced by round-the-world sailors in the Southern Ocean. This piece of hyperbole still gets wheeled out from time to time when commentators get a bit excited by big waves.

Piss The sea. See *green room*
We rolled to windward and all got dunked in the piss.
Stop that lazy sheet from dragging in the piss.

Pissing See *hosing*

Sheep in the paddock Breaking waves. See *white caps*
There are a few sheep in the paddock now.

Slop Small or moderate waves, in an irregular pattern,

causing the boat to roll around.

It was a bit sloppy out there tonight.

Washing machine Confused seas caused by the wind blowing against the flow of the tide, or by multiple wakes from power boats, ferries etc. Particularly common on the edge of America's Cup courses, where hundreds of spectator boats mill about and churn up the ocean.

It's like a washing machine out here today.

White caps Breaking waves. Also *white ones, white horses*. Waves generally start to break when the breeze reaches around 15 knots at sea, although fresh water starts to chop up at around 12 knots. This is why Lake Taupo often looks so inhospitable, and only the hardiest souls go sailing there.

Stuffed!

When the bow of the boat is driven into a wave, the helmsman can be said to have *stuck it in*, *stuffed it in* or *buried it*.

We were going downwind and he fully stuffed it into a wave.

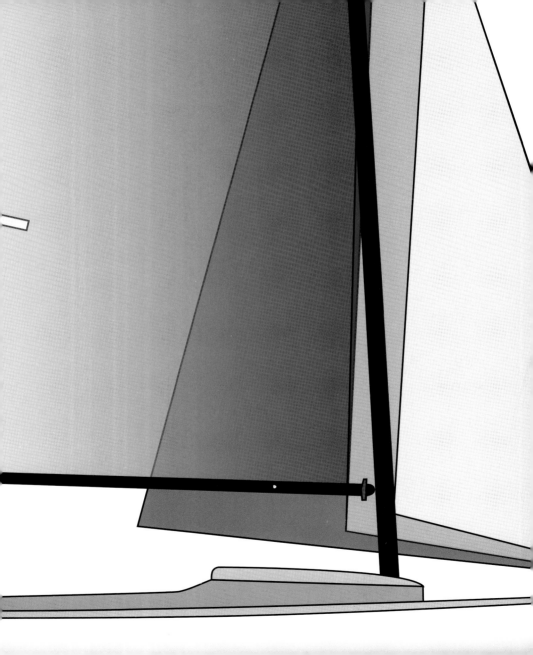

What are they doing?

Basic sailing manoeuvres

Let's go back to basics again to learn the terms for the standard sailing manoeuvres, before moving on to the more technical language used in yacht racing.

Wind

Head-to-wind

On the wind

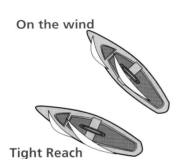

On the wind

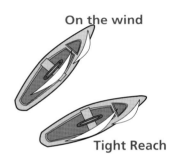

Tight Reach

Tight Reach

Points of sail

Beam reach

Beam reach

Broad reach

Broad reach

Sailing flat off/running

You should remember *port* and *starboard*; now there are a few other fundamental concepts and terms to grasp.

Windward The side of the boat closest to the wind, or referring to something in this direction, e.g. the *windward sheet.* Also known as the *weather* side.

Leeward The side of the boat away from the wind, e.g. the *leeward rail.* Note: Pronounced *loo*-ard.

Up and down

Alternating course to sail closer to where the wind is coming from is referred to as *going (or coming) up.* Sailing further away from where the wind is coming from is called *going down* or *bearing away.* In a yacht steered with a tiller, the helmsman pushes the tiller down to come up, and pulls it up to go down. But of course!

Sailing upwind

Sailing upwind means sailing as close as possible to the direction the wind is blowing from. Yachts cannot sail directly into the wind; they have to sail on an angle of around 40 degrees to it, so the wind flowing across the sails propels the boat forward. This is also called sailing

65

to windward, to weather, close-hauled (because the sails are pulled tight in), *on the wind* and *hard on* (the wind).

Sailing downwind

Once a yacht is sailing at a greater angle than around 40 degrees to the wind, and the sails are no longer sheeted right in, it is said to be sailing *off the wind* or *downwind* (but, counterintuitively, not *sailing to leeward*). Sailing at any angle from around 45 degrees to nearly 180 degrees to the wind is called *reaching*. There are many different types of reaches, from the *tight reach*, which is only just off the wind, to a *beam reach* (90 degrees to the wind) and *broad reach*. Sailing directly downwind, with the wind blowing right over the stern, is called *running*, or sailing *flat off.*

Tacking and gybing

Sailing a course to windward involves zigzagging, with the bow of the boat passing directly into the wind on each change of direction. This is known as *tacking, going about* or, in the US, *coming about*, and the action of making ground to windward by tacking is called *beating*. A boat's course to windward on each zig of the zag is

Wind

Tacking

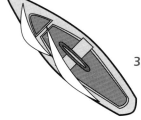

3. Starboard tack

2. Helm over,
passing through
head-to-wind

1. On the wind, port tack

called a *tack* (e.g. *the starboard tack* is when the wind is coming over the starboard side of the yacht) or *board* (*That yacht is still on the other board*). A yacht cannot be said to be on the *starboard board*, however.

Surprisingly, there is only one word for changing direction while sailing downwind: *gybing* although in olden times it was called *wearing*, and the Americans spell it like it sounds, *jibing.* It is faster and can be less controlled than tacking, as the end of the boom, rather than the leading edge of the sails, passes through the eye of the wind, and it can flick over suddenly. In an economy of language, a yacht's downwind course is also called a *gybe* (e.g. *port gybe*).

When the helmsman is preparing to tack, they let the crew know by saying *ready to tack* or *ready about* and then, as they push the helm away, *tacking*. More old-fashioned types might say *lee-o* or *helm's down*. Those used to sailing single-handed boats or who assume their crew are psychic might go straight to *tacking* without warning, or just tack without saying anything. Likewise, it is polite and, in most cases, vital to warn the crew when you are about to gybe, by saying *ready to gybe* or *set up to gybe*, then *gybing* or *gybe-o*.

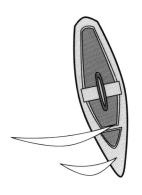

Wind

Gybing

1. Port gybe

2. Boom passes through the eye of the wind

3. Starboard gybe

Windward-leewards

Events such as the America's Cup use a *windward-leeward* (remember, pronounced *loo*-ard) course, where the yachts *beat* to a windward mark, then sail back downwind towards where they started from. They may complete several laps. Sailing this kind of course is known as *doing windward-leewards*. Depending on the wind conditions, the yachts may either *run* dead downwind, or sail a zigzag downwind course from *reach* to reach under *gennaker*. This is called *sailing angles*.

More useful terms

Backwind When the wind starts to flow down the *leeward* side of the sail. Can be deliberate, as in backwinding the jib during a tack, or accidental, when the wind is shifting or the sail is trimmed incorrectly.

Bring it on See *trim on*

Crack Not a drug-related term. To *ease* the sails. Possibly imitative, from the sound of the sheet being let out on the winch.

Give it a bit of crack.

Ease the sheet a little.

I'm going to crack off.

I am going to bear away.

We were slightly cracked.

We were sailing on a two-sail reach with slightly eased sheets.

Cracking off Bearing away.

Depowering Slowing the yacht down, either by easing the sails or altering course. See *powering up*

Douse US term for *drop*.

Drop The opposite of a *hoist*, bringing the *spinnaker* or *gennaker* down. A time of much frenetic activity.

Ease The opposite of *trim on*: letting out a sheet.

Also not a drug-related term (see *crack*), and not to be confused with the old-time *seats of ease*, which was a euphemism for the *heads*.

Give it some ease.
Let the sail out.
Being given the ease.
Being dumped, either by one's crew or romantic partner.

Eased sheets Sailing on a *tight reach* or *two-sail*, with the sails slightly eased.

Feathering Deliberately sailing slightly too *high* (see page 76) when *on the wind*, to *depower* without having to *ease* the sails. See *pinching*

Footing off Bearing away.

Head-to-wind Exactly what it sounds like: the yacht's bow pointing directly into the breeze. The yacht passes through head-to-wind during each *tack*. Can lead to getting into *irons.*

Heating it up Altering course to sail higher, when off the wind. To be *hot* is to be sailing high (see *pointing*). See also *soaking.*

Let's heat it up a little.

Hiking Technique by which crewmembers on dinghies

and other small boats lean out over the side of the yacht, to try to balance it and make it lean over less, with their feet or ankles under *hiking straps*. Also called *stacking*, and therefore, *stacking straps*. See also *trapeze* (page 36).

Hoist To raise a sail. Usually referring to the raising of the *spinnaker* or *gennaker*. See also *drop, douse*

Irons Unfortunately for many yachting widows, when a Yachtie *gets into irons*, it doesn't mean he's about to start pressing his own shirts. A yacht is considered to be *in irons* when it loses steerage when *head-to-wind*, usually due to tacking too slowly. The boat stalls and becomes impossible to steer, and may start sailing backwards.

Luff Now those of you who have been paying attention will now put up your hands and say 'That's one of the sides of a sail.' Well done! But *luff* is also a verb, meaning to alter course to come up into the wind, or above *on the wind* to *head-to-wind*. When racing, a yacht may *luff* another yacht that is passing it to windward as a defensive manoeuvre, forcing them to sail *higher* and slowing them down.

Pinching Sailing slightly too *high* when *on the wind*.

May be accidental (*You're pinching a bit, you can afford to come away*) or deliberate (*We're going to have to pinch like hell to lay that mark*). Also called *bunched up*. See also *feathering*

Pointing Being able to sail very high when on the wind, without *pinching,* due to good trim or a boat's design attributes.

Those guys are pointing to the sky.
That yacht is sailing very high.
Can you bring the main on a bit more, I can't point.
I am unable to sail on the wind without the mainsail sheeted in.

Powering up Bringing the sails on or altering course to increase the yacht's speed. See *depowering*

Rolling

1. The physical action of the boat rolling from side to side, especially when sailing *flat off* under *spinnaker*.

We've got a bit of a roll on.

2. Tacking the boat in light conditions by moving all the crew weight to windward, then back to the new windward side once the tack is complete, making the boat smoothly roll around onto the other tack. Called a *roll tack*.

Let's roll it.

3. To pass another yacht to windward, through superior size or speed, thus taking their breeze.

They're going to roll us.

Shy kite A *tight reach* under spinnaker.

Slightly cracked See *cracking off, eased sheets*

Soaking Altering course to sail *lower*, when off the wind.

I'm trying to soak down in these puffs.

Can you get a bit more soak?

Stacking See *hiking*

Strapped Sailing with the sails in too tightly.

We're a bit strapped.

Also, deliberately bringing the *spinnaker* or *gennaker* on tight and sailing as *high* as possible.

Let's just strap it on and stick it up there.

Taking up *Luffing* a boat to windward.

Let's take them up.

Trim on To pull a sheet in, to position the sail closer to the wind. The opposite of *ease*. Sometimes reduced to the command *trim!* (see *Things people yell,* pages 117–120)

Two-sail A *tight reach* under *mainsail* and *jib*. Can also be used as a verb.

We were two-sailing along nicely.

The concept of height

76

How close to the wind a boat can sail is referred to as its *height*. A boat which is sailing very close to the wind is said to be sailing *high*. Logically, if it not sailing very high, it is said to be *low*. The ideal combination when sailing upwind is to be *high and fast*, so you sail less distance to the mark, at a good speed, rather than *low and slow*. However, if *pinching*, it is possible to be *high and slow*, and if the sheets are slightly eased you are likely to be *low and fast*.

We've just got no height.
We are unable to sail very close to the wind.
They've got lots of height on us.
That other boat is able to sail much closer to the wind.

Avoiding a wine glass

The *spinnaker* or *gennaker* has to be carefully prepared for hoisting, packed in a bag in a special way to avoid the possibility of it being twisted around itself on the next hoist, known as a *wine glass*. While *packing the kite* the *bowman* (or whoever they have bribed to do it) runs their hands along at least two of its three edges, to make sure they are not entangled. This is called *running the tapes*.

Did you run the tapes?

Have you checked that the spinnaker packed correctly?

Things that go wrong

Broach When the yacht leans or is blown over uncontrollably, side-on to the wind because the sails are not adequately eased on a *reach*, or after a *gybe*. Usually followed by a *round up*.

Chinese gybe A very bad scene. An out-of-control situation in which the mainsail gybes suddenly but the spinnaker doesn't, resulting in a messy *broach* and *round up*, and usually lots of shouting and swearing. A boat to which this is happened is said to have *Chinesed*.

We were just reaching along beside them when they suddenly Chinesed.

Hitting the bricks Running aground on something hard, e.g. rocks.

Hitting the putty Running aground on something soft, e.g. mud or sand.

Laying over A peaceful-sounding term meaning the yacht is being blown over onto its side. See *broach*.

On its ear The yacht is *laid over* severely, usually following a *broach*.

Round up When the yacht's bow comes up into the wind in an uncontrolled fashion.

We got hit by a puff and rounded up.

Skid, doing a *Winding out* with the *spinnaker* or *gennaker* up. See also *broach*

Tea bag See *windward roll*

Trawling Dragging part of the *spinnaker* or *gennaker*, usually the *foot*, in the water while dropping it. Acts as a sea anchor, drastically slowing or stopping the yacht, as well as possibly damaging the sail. Called *shrimping* in the US.

Wind out A *broach* followed by a *round up*. (And that's wind as in winding a watch, not wind as in breeze.)

Windward roll When the yacht rolls to windward unexpectedly, due to there being too much crew weight to windward or sailing into a *hole* or another boat's *wind shadow.* On *trapeze* boats, this often results in the crew being *tea bagged* — dipped into the water on the end of their strings.

Wipe out See *broach*

Nautical superstitions

Due to the unpredictable and uncontrollable nature of the sea, sailors are traditionally superstitious. While not too many people nowadays have to deal with unruly albatrosses, here are some more common Yachtie superstitious you may encounter:

When launching a boat, it is bad luck if the champagne bottle doesn't break the first time it hits the boat In order to avoid this happening, many owners pre-cut a groove around the bottle to make sure it breaks. Interestingly, it took three attempts and two different bottles to launch SUI-91, one of Alinghi's new boats for the 2007 America's Cup.

Lucky clothing The most famous example of lucky clothing in New Zealand is the late Sir Peter Blake's red socks. Blake wore them during Team New Zealand's successful 1995 America's Cup campaign, and again during its 2000 defence, when it seemed the whole country was wearing them. Many Yachties seem to have lucky hats, lucky shirts, or even lucky undies (although this usually relates to action off the water).

80

It is bad luck to change a boat's name Stories abound of disastrous events which have befallen yachts which have been renamed. Apparently, this hoodoo can be broken by getting a virgin to urinate in the yacht's bilge, but this can be problematic for a number of reasons. It is also said to be bad luck to name a ship after a woman who is engaged to be married, as this will make the sea jealous, or to name a boat after your wife, as she will get it in the divorce.

Women are bad luck on boats Yeah, yeah — this sounds like something the boys made up as an excuse to go sailing with their mates. But this long-standing nautical tradition apparently relates to the fact that boats are considered to be female, and having another woman on board could make the boat jealous. For some inexplicable reason, however, it's OK if the woman is bare-breasted. Now *that* sounds like something the boys made up . . . but it explains the brazenness of many old-time figureheads.

Setting out on a voyage on a Friday is bad luck Launching a boat on a Friday is also said to bring bad luck. And there's that thing about the thirteenth, as well . . . There is an apocryphal story about a boat which was called *Friday*, launched on a Friday, which set off on its maiden voyage on a Friday, captained by a man named Friday — and was never seen again.

81

Bananas are bad luck on board a boat This one seems to have come across from the big book of fishing superstitions, but many Yachties believe bananas on board are bad luck when racing. However, some people swear banana cake is OK. Especially if it has cream cheese icing.

It is bad luck to paint a yacht green Or blue, apparently. And black seems to be of varying merit.

Seeing dolphins is good luck But seeing a whale is only good luck if it's not right under your bow.

Advanced Yachtie

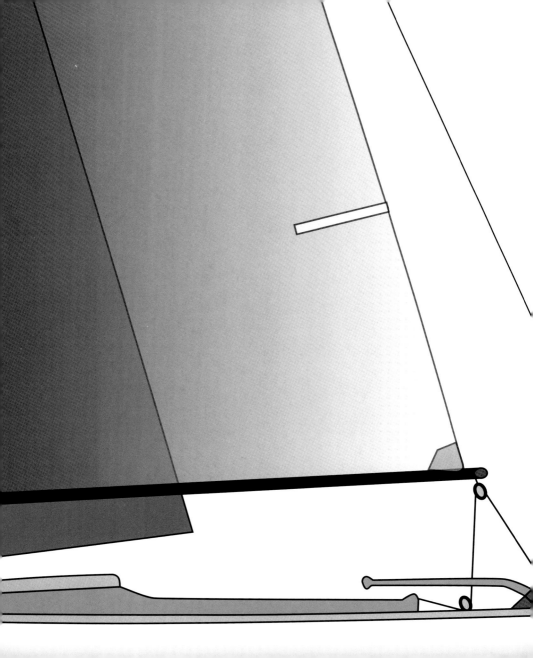

Ready to race

Once you have mastered Basic Yachtie, and you know your coaming from your galley and your midbowman from your runners, it's time to talk racing. Competitive sailing introduces a new set of vocabulary to Basic Yachtie, whether it is a twilight friendly series, or a serious international event such as the Olympics or the America's Cup.

What all racing events have in common is that there will be a *start sequence*, during which the *race committee* counts down to firing the *start gun*. Yachts then cross the *startline* and complete a course around a series of *marks* or *buoys* before crossing the *finish line*. But of course a whole lot of other stuff happens in between.

Race management

Black flag 1. When the race committee gets sick of running *recalls*, it may fly the *black flag*. This means yachts that are over the *startline* when the *gun* goes are automatically disqualified rather than being able to duck back behind the line before starting.

2. A boat being black flagged by the *on-the-water umpires* in match racing means instant disqualification for some serious misdemeanour. See also *round the ends*

Blue Peter Not something male sailors get during cold winter series races, but a blue flag with a white square in the centre, flown during the start sequence. Hoisted at four minutes before the start and dropped at one minute under the current protocol. Also called the *preparatory* or *P.*

Committee boat Boat on which the *race committee* is

based, from which racing is started and finished. Usually forms one end of the *startline*.

Double Winning a race both on *line* (i.e. first to finish) and *handicap* (corrected time). The cause of much justifiable pride.

We got the double.

Early Over the startline before the start gun is fired.

Damn it, we're early.

Five-minute The *start sequence* for many races is five minutes long. There are often sound signals at four minutes and one minute to the start. These terms are used as names. Also called the *warning signal*.

That was the four-minute [gun].

We're within the five-minute.

Gun A sound signal, made to start the race and when the winning boat crosses the finish line. Often now a hooter rather than a blank fired from an actual shotgun, but saying *We got the hooter tonight* doesn't sound quite the same. Leads to the expression *the gun boat*, which is the boat which wins a particular race or has a habit of doing so. Sometimes also *bullet*.

They got the gun again tonight.

They won the race.

We got three bullets.
We won three races.

Handicap A mysterious and largely inexplicable system whereby a boat's elapsed time (the time it takes to complete the race) is multiplied by a time-correction factor (effectively a percentage) reflecting the boat's size and typical performance. This is supposed to give all boats an equal chance of winning the race. However, it is often the cause of much discussion and bewilderment.

Line The first boat to finish the race (and get the *gun*) is said to have won *on line*. See *handicap, double*

OD/OOD Abbreviation for *officer of the day*, the member of the *race committee* in charge of running the racing.

Pre-start The period between the *warning signal* and when the *start gun* is fired in a *match race*. This can be the most critical and often the most interesting time of an America's Cup race, when the yachts are in close proximity and are actively trying to attack each other. Commentators get very excited during this phase, as *winning the start* — not necessarily crossing the start line first, but in the best position relative to your opponent — often decides who wins the race.

Preparatory See *Blue Peter*

Race committee Often a team of weathered old salts who are in charge of running the racing. To be treated with the utmost respect. See *OD*

Recall Yachts that are over the *startline* when the *gun* goes will be *recalled* to start again. Recalls can be *individual*, when just one or two boats are over, or *general*, when the whole fleet is restarted.

Round the ends Rule which means yachts that are over the *startline* when the *gun* goes have to sail around the ends of the line (around the *committee boat* or *start mark*) and re-cross the *startline* before starting the race.

Start boat See *committee boat*

Start gun See *gun*

Start mark See *startline*

Start sequence A ritual of noises and flags conducted by the race committee to count down to the firing of the *start gun*. The current international sequence for fleet racing is to make a sound signal (usually firing a *gun* or sounding an air horn) at five minutes, four minutes and one minute to the start time, then one to signal the start of the race. All yachts must be behind the *startline* when the *start gun* is fired. In *match racing*, this period is known as the *pre-start* and is a critical time tactically.

Start-finish line See *startline*

Startline An imaginary line running between the *committee boat* and a *start mark*, usually set at right angles to the wind direction so the yachts start on the wind. Sometimes the same line may be used for the start and the finish of the race, in which case it is called, cleverly, the *start-finish line.*

Warning signal See *five-minute*

Wind

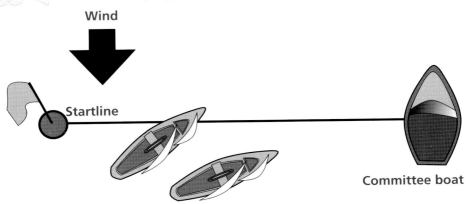

Startline

Committee boat

Swearing

There are no two ways about it, swearing is a major aspect of Yachtie — especially Advanced or Racing Yachtie. It seems bizarre that a language with so many fascinating variables and intriguing expressions should sometimes be reduced to such unimaginative basics but sometimes, especially in stressful situations, expletives seem to be the only words that come to mind.

As well as the usual gamut of low-grade swear words, Yachtie speakers seem particularly enamoured of the f-word, which can be used as an expletive (*F*ck! The kite halyard's jammed!*), a modifier (*That f*cking kite halyard's jammed!*), a noun (*Can you pull that f*cker on a bit*), a verb (*I think that halyard's a bit f*cked*), or, in extreme situations, a combination of the above (*F*ck, the f*cking f*cker's f*cked!*).

Don't feel that you have to swear to speak Yachtie; just don't be horrified if everyone else does.

shoot the Breeze

Ready to race

Pre-start manoeuvres

In America's Cup racing, the pre-start is a rich source of Yachtie vocab. You may hear commentators refer to the following:

Box See *entering the box*

Circling When the two boats perform a series of *tacks* and *gybes* to sail a roughly circular course. A yacht may circle to kill time before the start, or to try to gain an advantage over its opponent.

Contact Euphemism for a collision.
Ooh, there's been some contact there.
One yacht has just hit the other.

Cut See *killing speed*

Dead in the water As serious as America's Cup racing becomes, there is no recorded instance of a skipper actually killing their opponent. However, a boat which has low or no speed, especially after or during pre-start manoeuvres, is said to be *dead in the water*.

Engaging When the two competing yachts come together in the *box* and interact, forcing each other to *tack* or *gybe* away.

Entering the box The *box* is an imaginary square downwind of the *startline*. In *match racing*, the yachts must enter this pre-start area from opposite ends of the startline, within a specified time frame. The yacht which enters the box from the starboard end of the line has initial right-of-way, and has the opportunity to *hunt* its opposition once the yachts *engage*.

Favoured end Although the *startline* is supposed to be set at right angles to the wind, if the wind shifts slightly it can become biased. The *favoured end* of the line is the end closer to the *top mark*. The yacht that starts at the favoured end is likely to do better on the *first beat*, as it technically has a shorter distance to sail to the *top mark*.

Neither end of the line is particularly favoured.
The startline has been set well, at right angles to the wind direction.

Hunting When one yacht uses its right-of-way to force its opponent into an unfavourable position. The right-of-way yacht can chase the other away from the *startline*, or to the *unfavoured end* of the startline.

Killing speed If a yacht is going to cross the *startline* too early, or for other tactical reasons, the skipper might make the call to *kill speed*. They will either steer up into the wind (avoiding *getting into irons*) or call for the sails to be *cut* (let right out).

Tagging *Contact* between boats is highly discouraged by the racing rules. However, sometimes to make a point, a skipper will give their opposition a slight nudge or *tag* them. Vigorous protest-flag waving will then ensue, usually by both parties, to encourage the umpires to award a penalty.

Unfavoured end See *favoured end*

Winning the start It is often said that the boat that wins the start usually goes on to win the race. However, unless one yacht completely cleans out its opposition and leaves them *dead in the water*, being over the *startline* first doesn't necessarily mean a win is assured. In fact, in the 2003 Louis Vuitton Cup series in Auckland, the yacht that nominally won the start only won the race 51% of the time.

Scoring terms

You may see the following acronyms on the score sheet of a racing series or regatta.

OCS On Course Side. The yacht was over the startline when the gun was fired. The abbreviation used to be PMS (for premature start) but some women got irrationally upset about it.

DNC did not compete

DNS did not start

DNF did not finish

DSQ disqualified

DFL dead f*cking last

Many of the following terms and tactics are commonly used in the America's Cup and other match racing regattas, but many of them will come in handy when fleet racing, too.

Fleet racing vs. match racing

There are two main types of yacht racing: *fleet racing*, in which a number of boats all start the race at the same time, and *match racing*, which is a race between two boats of the same type. The America's Cup is a match racing regatta, although some fleet racing has now been introduced to the preliminary rounds. Match racing has slightly different rules from fleet racing, as well as some special manoeuvres and terms not heard elsewhere in Yachtie.

97

Sailing upwind

Banging the corner Sailing all the way out to one or other *layline* (see *Getting laid*, page 108) before tacking for the *mark*.

Bouncing When the *controlling* yacht forces their opposition to *tack* by tacking on top of them or asserting right-of-way, essentially sending them back where they came from.

They've just been bounced right out of there.

Controlling Being in the right-of-way position (e.g. on *starboard tack*) and able to force the opposition to tack or sail on the less *favoured side* of the course. See also *protecting a side*

Covering In its simplest form, *covering* is staying between your competition and the next mark. This means not letting them sail off into another area of the course, going with them if they try to do so and you think they might gain an advantage, and tacking in sync with them to neutralise any gains they might make. Can either be a *tight cover* if your opposition is nearby, or a *loose cover* if they are some way back or there are several boats to keep an eye on.

Cross When two yachts sailing towards each other on opposite tacks meet. Under the racing rules, the yacht on starboard tack has right-of-way, while the yacht on port may have to tack away or *dip*.

Are they going to cross?

Are they going to be clear ahead of us when our courses meet?

Dip When two yachts *cross* upwind, if the yacht on port cannot pass clear astern of the starboard-tack boat, it either has to *tack* onto the other board to give way or *ease sheets* and *bear away* slightly to dip its stern.

Dummy tack A tricky manoeuvre whereby a yacht sets up for and pretends to be starting to tack, to try to force its opposition to tack to *cover*. Can also be used as a verb (*They just got dummied into tacking*). See also *tacking duel*.

Facial See *sitting on their face*

Favoured side Due to the fickle nature of the breeze, one side of the course (port or starboard as you look upwind) is likely to be more favourable to sail up. There might be stronger breeze, less tide or greater likelihood of encountering a *lift*. Before the start, the crew ascertains which side of the course is likely to be favoured by observing the conditions and other boats. See also *protecting a side*, *favoured end* (page 94).

First beat The first windward leg of the race, to the *top mark*. This can be a critical period in match racing, as it reveals who picked the *favoured side* of the course in the *pre-start*.

First cross A critical indicator of who has the

upper hand in the early stages of an America's Cup race. When the yachts are on opposite tacks, it can be hard to tell who is ahead, until they come together and *cross*. The boat which crosses ahead is in the *controlling* position, as it can then *cover* its opposition.

Gauge The relative distance between two boats that are on the same board.

They're really opening up some gauge.

Lee bow Tacking to *leeward* of an opposing yacht, slightly overlapped. The leeward yacht can then *luff* their opposition, or force them to tack away because of the *dirty air* being generated off the back of their sails. See *sitting on their face, slam dunk*

Loose cover See *cover*

Protecting a side A yacht sailing on the *favoured side* of the course might try to protect its advantage by *covering* its opposition, or *bouncing* them back towards the middle of the course.

Shut out When a yacht is prevented from sailing where it wants to go, either in the *pre-start* or when approaching the mark, by the actions of the right-of-way boat.

They've just shut them right out.

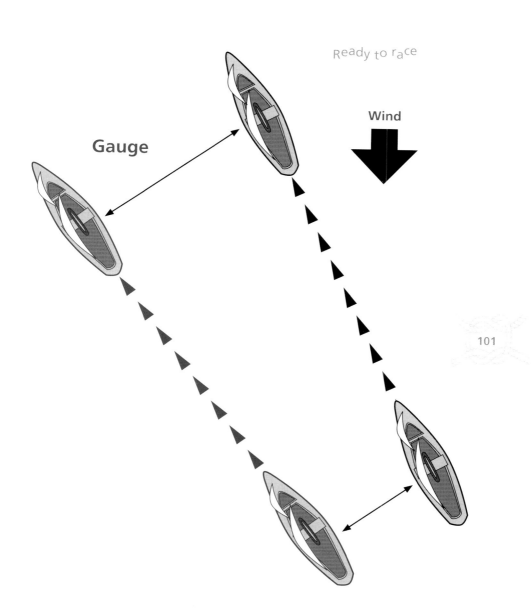

Wind

Gauge

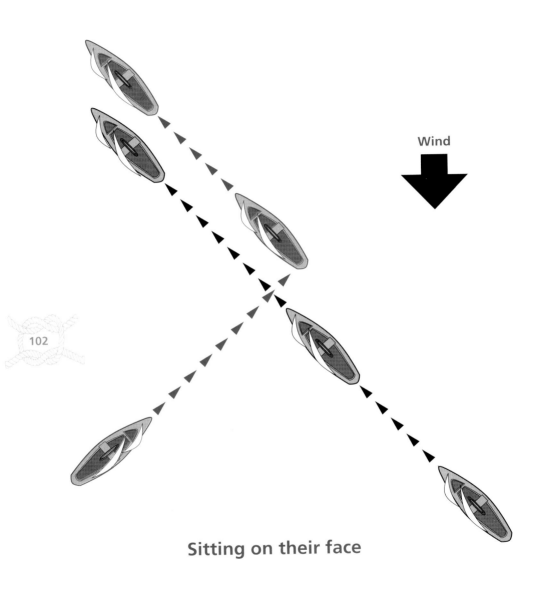

Wind

Sitting on their face

102

Sitting on their face Tacking to windward of an opposing yacht, slightly overlapped. The windward yacht is in a *controlling* position, as the *leeward* boat can't tack away: they just have to sail slowly in the windward boat's *dirty air* until they are clear astern and can tack. You probably won't hear this one used in TV commentary, but you'll know what's going on. Also called *giving them a facial.* See also *slam dunk, lee bow*

Slam dunk Tacking right in front of an opposing yacht, so they are forced to slow down, bear away or tack. As with *sitting on their face,* the leading yacht is in the *controlling* position. See also *lee bow*

Split tacks Two yachts sailing on opposite tacks, away from each other. Sometimes in match racing there will be a *split tack start*, with one yacht going one way and its opposition the other — a slightly risky manoeuvre, as one boat is likely to be wrong.

Tacking duel Intense phase of a race where two boats engage in a series of tacks, either to try to break a *cover* or to *defend a side*. One yacht may eventually do a slow or bad tack, giving its opposition an advantage. Good for TV. See also *dummy tack*

Tight cover See *cover*

Getting around the buoys

The course for any yacht race is defined in terms of a series of *marks* that have to be gone around, in a certain order and direction (e.g. *taken to starboard* — the buoy must be on the starboard side of the yacht). Sometimes these are inflatable marks or buoys that have been specially laid (in which case they are called *laid marks*), or the course can be set around existing features such as channel markers or other navigation buoys.

It is against the rules to hit a mark while rounding it (see *Protests and penalties,* page 116), not to mention expensive if it is one of those big steel jobs they use to mark the channel for container ships . . .

Traditional Olympic yacht racing courses are a triangular shape, with the yachts beating to a *top mark* (or *windward mark*), reaching to a *wing mark* (or *gybe mark*), gybing, then reaching on the other angle to the *bottom mark*, completing several laps and often including a *windward-leeward* leg.

Windward-leeward courses (see page 70) are used for match racing events such as the America's Cup. For the 2007 America's Cup, a *gate* will be laid instead of a single bottom mark. This means there will be a pair of

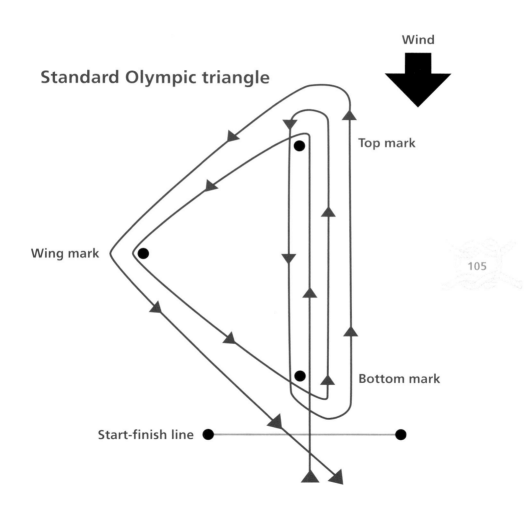

Wind

Standard Olympic triangle

Top mark

Wing mark

Bottom mark

Start-finish line

buoys between which the yachts must pass, rounding either buoy them before heading off upwind again. In windward-leeward fleet racing, sometimes a gate can be set instead of a single *top mark*, to encourage the fleet to separate.

Also, sometimes in windward-leeward racing an *offset mark* will be laid near to the *top mark*, introducing a short reaching leg or *dogleg* before the downwind leg.

There is also a complicated set of rules relating to right-of-way when boats come together to round a mark. This may result in some shouting if one or other yacht believes its rights are being infringed (see *Things people yell*, page 117).

Calling the mark Many a novice sailor has been caught out by the helmsman's seemingly unintelligible request *Call the mark for me.* The correct response is not *What would you like me to call it?* but *Three boat lengths away, ten degrees down* (or whatever the appropriate range and bearing may be). Often when approaching a rounding mark the helmsman won't be able to see it behind the headsail, and will require a crewmember to tell them how far away it is, so they can steer as close to it as possible without hitting it.

Wind

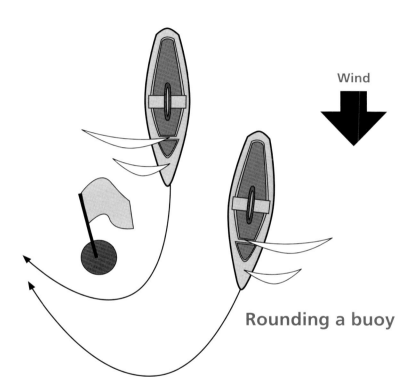

Rounding a buoy

Shooting the mark If, coming into the mark, the helmsman find he can't quite *lay* it, he may *luff up* and try to let the boat's momentum carry it around. This can end in disaster, especially if the tide is pushing the yacht down on to the mark.

Getting laid

Yachties will frequently talk in terms of *laying* a mark. When a yacht is sailing on a course that will take them in a straight line to the next turning mark, it is said to be *laying* or *on the lay*.

Calling the lay Letting the helmsman know when the yacht is on the *layline*, and can tack and lay the mark.

Easy lay A comfortable course to the mark.

Layline An imaginary line running directly to the mark, on the angle the yacht is sailing on (e.g. at around 40 degrees to the wind when sailing on the wind). A yacht sailing on the layline can sail straight to the mark without having to tack or gybe.

Are we laying?

Will we get to the mark without altering course?

Marginal lay May not be able to lay the mark.

Overlaid Sailing above the *layline.*

We've overlaid — crack off a bit and reach down to it.

Underlaid Tacking too soon, to sail below the *layline.*

Dammit, we've underlaid — we're going to have to pinch.

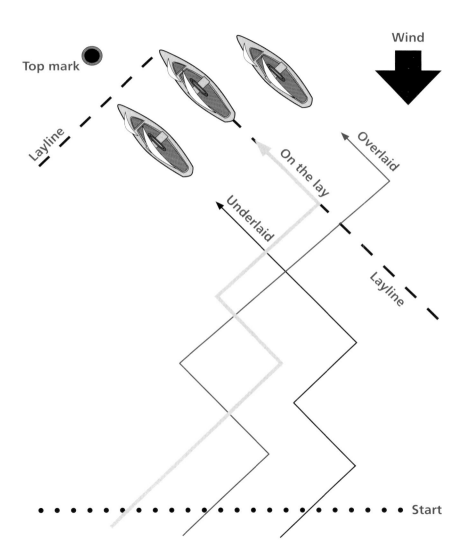

Wind

Top mark

Layline

Overlaid

On the lay

Underlaid

Layline

Start

Sailing downwind

Bearaway set See *set*

Blanket See *covering*

Covering Covering downwind is different from covering upwind, as it is the trailing boat has the advantage. If the yachts are close enough, the trailing boat can *blanket* the downwind yacht, positioning itself between the wind and the leading boat so it receives less wind and slows down. As America's Cup races finish downwind, this can mean some last-minute upsets.

Dip-pole gybe On America's Cup and some other larger yachts, one end of the spinnaker pole is attached to a track on the mast. When the spinnaker is gybed, the outboard end of the pole is unclipped from the *brace* and is swung down and across the bow, then clipped onto the old sheet, which has now become the brace (remember?). Spinnaker poles on smaller boats have clips on both ends, so the pole is *end-for-ended* in the *gybe*, rather than one end staying fixed.

Douse US term for *drop.*

Drop Bringing down the spinnaker or gennaker. The sail is usually dropped on the leeward side, but there are other permutations: see windward drop, *poleless drop, gybe*

drop, float drop, Kiwi drop.

End-for-end See *dip-pole gybe*

Float drop See *poleless drop*

Gybe drop Drop in which the spinnaker pole is removed, the mainsail is gybed and the spinnaker dropped on the new windward side. Also known as the *Kiwi drop*, after the manouevre was brought to world prominence at the 1987 America's Cup by the crew of KZ7. We'd been doing it for years.

Gybe set See *set*

Human pole See *poleless drop*

Kiwi drop See *gybe drop*

Luffing match On the downwind leg of a match race, if the yachts are close enough together they can engage in a *luffing match*, in which the leeward boat tries to *take up* its opponent, slowing them down and upsetting their spinnaker trim.

Mexican takedown US term for *Kiwi drop*. There is also apparently a *reverse Mexican*, which sounds like what happens after a hard night on the tequila.

Poleless drop A spinnaker drop in which the spinnaker pole is removed before the drop. A crewmember acts as a *human pole* and holds out the corner of the spinnaker to keep it filled until it is time to drop it. Useful if the helmsman wants to gybe right at the mark, once the drop is complete, or tack straight after the rounding. See also *gybe drop*.

Poleless hoist Setting the *spinnaker* without first attaching the *spinnaker pole*. Once the sail is set, the helmsman can then gybe and the pole can be attached on the new windward side. An alternative to the *gybe set*.

Reverse Mexican See *Mexican takedown*

Set Relating to the *spinnaker* or *gennaker*. The sail is said to be set when it is fully hoisted, filled with wind and nicely trimmed. The action of hoisting the sail is also called a set. A standard *spinnaker* set, where the yacht comes around the *top mark* and bears away, is called a *bearaway set* (simple). Likewise, if the skipper calls for a gybe immediately after the mark, then the hoist, or a *poleless hoist* followed by a quick *gybe*, this is called a *gybe set*. If this spinnaker is hoisted and the skipper gybes before anyone is ready for it, this is called a f*ck up.

Windward drop See *poleless drop*

Other useful terms

Barging Steering a yacht into a space between yachts, or between a yacht and a mark, into which it really can't fit. Not nice. Or allowed.

Buffalo girls A reference to the 1983 song by Malcolm McLaren. And what do buffalo girls do? Go round the outside.

There was a pile-up at the bottom mark so we went buffalo girls.

Bumper boats A minor collision. See also *T-bone*
They were playing bumper boats at the top mark.

Calling for room Not the same as calling *get a room!* when two of your crewmembers are pashing up a storm after a few rums back at the yacht club (although this is a very handy phrase in this situation). A boat which has right-of-way when approaching a *mark* may signal to another boat that it must be allowed space to round the mark (see *Buoy room!*, page 117).

Calling for rum What the skipper may do after a particularly tight race or close call. Or maybe just on the downwind leg because they are feeling a little thirsty.

Calling for water Indicating to another boat that they need to get out of the way or you are going to run

113

aground. Often hotly contested and debated boat-to-boat. Can be a trap for young players: I recently heard a story about a keen young crewmember who, hearing the skipper yelling *I need water, I need water* obligingly went below and got him a bottle of water. Needless to say, this person will never be allowed to forget this gaffe.

Calling the breeze Not like calling the cat: you can't make the breeze come to you, no matter how much you might want it to. Rather, this means looking at the pattern of the wind on the water and telling the helmsman and trimmers what's going to happen, and when, e.g. *Breeze on in five* or *Bit of a flat spot then a sharp puff in ten [seconds]*. If it's *puffy*, also called *calling the puffs*.

Cluster Short for *cluster f*ck*. A major problem, or collection of connected problems.
We had a total cluster at the bottom mark when the kite wouldn't come down.

Inside To be between a competing yacht and a mark
We've got the inside running at the bottom mark.

Money in the bank Ground gained to windward on a reaching leg, in preparation for the possibility that you might have to *bear away* later if *knocked* or if the breeze increases. A good thing to have.

Rhumbline   Not the queue at the yacht club bar, but a navigation term meaning a course that represents the most direct route or shortest distance between two marks of the course. The yacht club being the nautical equivalent of golf's nineteenth hole, however, the rhumbline could also be the shortest distance between the finish line and the bar.

Rule 69   Strangely, this is the international rule covering gross misconduct either on or off the water. Being protested under this rule can result in the sailor being banned.

They should be 69ed for that.

That was an unsportsmanlike act.

T-bone   A major collision, whereby one boat hits another bow-on, amidships. In this situation, one boat usually has right-of-way and the other boat is horribly wrong — and it's not always the one that got hit.

They just came in at pace and t-boned them.

We've got a bit on   Classic understatement, meaning in fact that all sorts of things are going wrong. I am also fond of the extended metaphor *More on than the early settlers.*

Yachtie   The yacht club. Where many lies are told and stories amplified.

Protests and penalties

Yacht racing is governed by a complex set of rules governing right-of-way and other behaviour. In regular fleet racing, if a crew knows they have broken a rule (including touching a mark during a rounding), they can exonerate themselves by completing one or more *penalty turns* (known as a *360* or *720*). However, if they feel another crew has broken a rule, and that crew does not perform a penalty, a *protest* has to be lodged after the race. This will then be heard in a mini courtroom hearing at a later date, and either dismissed or one of the boats disqualified from the race.

In America's Cup and other match racing, to make the racing more immediate and understandable for television viewers with short attention spans, *on-the-water umpires* follow the pairs of boats and make rulings on the spot. If one yacht thinks the other has broken a rule, they vigorously wave the *Y flag* (which has red and yellow diagonal stripes). The umpires will consider the infringement, then hold up a *green flag* if they consider there was no incident, or a *blue* or *yellow flag* to indicate which of the two yachts has been awarded a penalty. Unlike fleet racing, in match racing penalty turns do not have to be taken as soon as possible; they can be saved up and done at a tactically convenient time. A yacht can also be given the *black flag*, which means instant disqualification.

117

Things people yell

In the heat of the moment in a yacht racing situation, fluent Yachtie speakers may lapse into their native tongue and start yelling unintelligible commands. Keep your head (while all around you are losing theirs) and listen out for the following:

Brace! Pull on the brace. Not *Assume the brace position — we're going to crash.*

Bum cleat! Someone is sitting on a sheet or control line, effectively cleating it with their buttocks.

Buoy room! If two yachts are overlapped within two

boat-lengths of a mark of the course, the boat on the outside is entitled to give the inside boat room to round the mark. Often hotly contested. See *no room!*

Do your turns! We believe you have broken a rule and need to complete *penalty turns* to exonerate yourself, or we are going to *protest.*

Dump! Let the sheet out big-time — see *ease!* Many arguments have ensued between skipper and crew about the difference between these two terms:

> ***Ease it! I said ease it!***
> *I am easing it!*
> ***I meant dump it!***
> *But you said ease it! etc etc*

If you are making the call, try to be as precise as you can: even fluent Yachtie speakers are seldom mind-readers.

Ease! Let the sheet out. See *dump!*

Fence! See *skirt!*

Halyard! Pull on the *halyard* (whichever one is appropriate).

Heads! The boat is about to *gybe*; everyone keep their heads down so they don't get hit by the *boom.*

Made! Call given by the mastman when the *spinnaker halyard* has reached the top of the mast, or when the gybing of the *spinnaker pole* is complete. The *bowman* or *trimmer* may then call *set!* when the *gennaker* has filled.

No room! We don't believe you have any rights to call for *buoy room*.

On! See *sheet!*

Protest! You have broken a rule and we are going to lodge a protest against you. It is an official part of the protest procedure that the protesting boat must give a verbal signal to the infringing boat, to give it the opportunity to exonerate itself by doing *penalty turns*. In reality, instead of calling *We are protesting you*, the wronged crew usually yell things like *You can't do that! Do your turns! Right, we're protesting you, you bunch of ***** etc etc.

Room! See *buoy room!*

Set! See *made!*

Sheet! Trim on (i.e. pull on the sheet). Unless you are sailing with an Australian, in which case he may be swearing at you. May be used as a command by the *trimmer* to the *grinder*, in tandem with the command *hold*, i.e. *sheet* means the grinder is to winch the sail in, and *hold* means *stop winching until I tell you to winch again*.

Skirt! As the *genoa* is trimmed on after a tack, its *foot*

119

can get caught outside the *lifelines*. The call *skirt* or *fence* means *can a crewmember please go forward and flick the foot back inside the lifelines.*

Starboard! Called to an opposition yacht, sailing on port, to indicate right-of-way.

Tack! Pull on the *tackline* (note: not put the boat about).

Tail! Request for the *tailer* to do their job and pull some weight on the *sheet* so it can be winched in.

Trim! See *sheet!*

Up! Up! Steer a higher course. Yelled either to the skipper by the crew if the boat needs to come up to avoid an obstruction, or to a competing boat if it is being *luffed*.

Weight! The yacht feels unbalanced to the helmsman and one or more crewmembers need to move to change the angle of heel. More specifically, could be:

Weight up! One or more crewmember needs to move to windward to balance the yacht.

Weight out! Crewmembers need to *hike*, *stack* or otherwise get their weight outboard to flatten out the yacht.

Weight down! One or more crewmember needs to move to leeward to balance the yacht.

Please note, it's OK to shout to make sure commands are clearly heard by other crewmembers. It's not OK to just shout at people. No one wants to sail with a screamer.

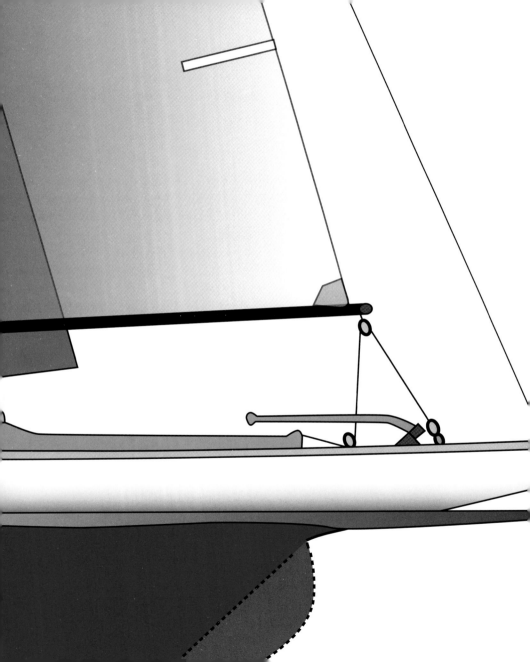

Did they say that out loud?

As observant readers will have noted, Yachtie is full of words and phrases familiar to the landlubber that mean something completely different when used at sea. There are a number of double entendres and, let's face it, downright dodgy sayings.

Here's a guide to some of the more inexplicable and slightly risqué phrases that you may hear uttered on board, along with what they *really* mean.

Are we going to lay that buoy?

Are we going to make the next mark without tacking?
(Note: this doesn't sound dodgy to Americans, not
because they don't have such a dirty sense of humour, but
because they pronounce buoy *boo-ey*. Which is funny in
itself.)

Are you hard on?

Are you sailing on the wind?

Can you get it in any further?

Can that sail be trimmed on any more? See *Is it
right in?*

Get the pole up.

Please get the spinnaker pole rigged for the hoist.

Give me some crack.

Please ease the sheet. See *Give me some ease*

Give me some ease.

Please ease the sheet. See *Give me some crack*

Give them a good hard luff.

Come up and luff the opposing boat. See *Take them up*

I think they're going for the dip pole.

The other boat is going to dip-pole gybe.

I think we need a bit of tweaker.

Please pull on the barberhauler.

I'm just cracking off a bit.
I am bearing away slightly.
Is it right in?
Is that sail trimmed right on? Also *Is it all the way in?*
See *Can you get it in any further?*
Just strap it on.
Trim the spinnaker or gennaker on tightly.
Let's throw a loose cover on them.
Let's sail between the opposing boat and the mark.
Man, those guys are hot.
That boat is sailing very high. Can also be used when
talking about Prada's America's Cup team.

Nice set! Lady sailors, do not be a) alarmed or b)
flattered if someone says this to you after a mark
rounding. It just means they think the kite went up well.
However, if someone says it to you in the bar afterwards,
beware.

Pinch your mother's arse!
Sail as high as you can.
Take them up!
Come up and luff the opposing boat. See *Give them a*
good hard luff

125

That looks like an easy lay.
We can sail to the mark without having to tack.
They've been sitting on our face the whole beat.
The other yacht is sailing to windward and taking our breeze.
They've got their prod out.
The other boat has extended its spinnaker prod.
We fully stuck it in that hole.
We sailed into an area of no breeze.
We're really high tonight.
We are able to sail very close to the wind.
We're sucking the big kumara here.
We're not doing very well.
We won't lay unless we're hard on.
We aren't going to make the buoy without tacking unless we sail on the wind.

Who's on keyboards? Not an invitation to discuss music, but a query regarding who is operating the pit, pulling up the *halyards* etc.

You can't stick it in there, pal.
You have no right-of-way or room.

Acknowledgements

Thanks to everyone I sail with for their contributions (witting and unwitting), but especially to the crew of *Manic*: Rob Shaw, Derek Saward, Jodi Fraser, Oliver Hawkley and Blair Gerrard. Thanks also to Amanda Hunt, for being an enthusiastic collector and appreciator of Yachtie expressions, and my parents, who first took me sailing as a child (even if I did take along a book to read!) Finally, and essentially, thank you to Jenny Hellen and Nic McCloy at Random House for being so enthusiastic about *Shoot the Breeze* and making it a reality, and Trevor Newman for his patience and his cool design.